Original title:
Under the Elm's Embrace

Copyright © 2025 Creative Arts Management OÜ
All rights reserved.

Author: Alec Donovan
ISBN HARDBACK: 978-1-80567-021-6
ISBN PAPERBACK: 978-1-80567-101-5

The Tranquil Refuge of Sylvan Shadows

Where squirrels play hide and seek,
A tree stands tall, quite unique.
It hums a tune with every breeze,
As critters chatter, enjoy their tease.

The roots are home to much delight,
A raccoon plans his nighttime flight.
With laughter ringing through the leaves,
The forest whispers all it weaves.

A Dance Amongst Twisted Limbs

Twisted branches sway and sway,
The birds all join the quirky play.
A plump old crow, he wobbles, too,
Sipping rain like fine brew.

The sun beams down with playful grins,
While bugs perform their tiny spins.
A caterpillar joins the jive,
In leafy grooves, they all will thrive.

Echoes in the Leafy Sanctuary

Beneath a bough, a nap is shared,
Twitching tails, no creature cared.
A chorus forms of snorts and snores,
As sleepy heads rest on old floors.

The breeze invites a tickle fight,
In sacred shades from morning light.
Chirps and chuckles fill the air,
It's just nature's grand affair.

Breath of the Olden Tree

The old tree sighs with wisdom rare,
It chuckles softly, unaware.
With every creak and moan it makes,
A laughter echoes, and joy awakens.

Its bark holds tales of days gone by,
Where frogs once croaked and fireflies fly.
A gathering place for all who roam,
It feels just like a laughing home.

The Canopy's Gentle Caress

In the shade, squirrels play,
Chasing thoughts of the day.
Acorns fall, plop and drop,
Nature's game will never stop.

Branches wiggle, leaves giggle,
Wind-swept dreams all seem to wiggle.
June bugs dance, unaware of chance,
In this leafy, silly romance.

Heartbeats in the Silhouette

Beneath the branches, whispers tease,
A raccoon bids, "Take it with ease!"
Sunlight filters, a spotlight's grace,
Critters join this quirky race.

With shadows stretching, laughter's clear,
A bunny hops, drawing near.
Lively shadows prance and glide,
In this playful sylvan ride.

Treetop Reveries and Grounded Roots

Up high, birdies sing with glee,
While ants march out for their tea.
Branches sway, a playful cue,
All nature's pranks, bit of a zoo.

Underfoot, worms spin yarns,
While butterflies flaunt their charms.
Each creature, in laughter, weaves,
A history told by rustling leaves.

Cradled by the Whispering Wind

The breeze hums tunes, soft and sweet,
As critters gather for a treat.
A snail glides slowly, takes his time,
While grasshoppers make up silly rhymes.

Clouds drift lazily, thoughts fly high,
A ladybug, dressed up, passes by.
In this nook, joy finds a way,
To turn an ordinary day into play.

Embracing Life Beneath the Canopy

Squirrels chat as acorns fall,
A dance of leaves in nature's hall.
Bees buzz loud, a busy crew,
Who knew they'd throw a picnic too?

Laughter rings in shadowed light,
With ants marching, what a sight!
The branches sway, a gentle tease,
As rabbits hop with such great ease.

A nap sounds good, I close my eyes,
But was that a joke or just some flies?
Dreams of pie drift on the breeze,
And now I'm hungry, if you please!

In this realm of tree and cheer,
It's hard to hold back a hearty leer.
For life's a game played full of jest,
Beneath the leaves, we too are blessed.

Green Dreams in the Quiet Hours

In the twilight glow we find our peace,
With crickets chirping, all worries cease.
A sleepy toad in a curious croak,
Makes friends with a raccoon, what a joke!

The moon peeks through the leafy lace,
As fireflies twinkle, a playful race.
Dreamers gather, sharing their rhymes,
In the soft laughter of distant chimes.

Whispers wander on the cool night air,
As owls hoot softly, beyond compare.
What was that noise? A falling nut?
Or just my friend tumbling on his butt?

Morning will come, with its golden hue,
But for now, we giggle at the dew.
In this grove where dreams collide,
We'll keep the laughter and joy inside.

Silence Speaks Among the Branches

In the hush where wise trees grow,
A snail slides by, moving so slow.
With mismatched socks, I paint a scene,
Who knew nature could be so keen?

A squirrel wears a tiny cap,
While beneath me, a sleepy gap.
I ponder life, its silly ways,
The whispers of leaves, in playful gaze.

The chatter of bugs, in secret code,
Discussing things on this merry road.
A frog just leaped with a terrific splash,
And now I'm wet, but what a laugh!

Let's toast to moments, big and small,
With laughter echoing through it all.
In stillness found, there's joy to share,
Among these branches, we're quite the pair.

A Refuge Where Spirits Gather

In this hideout, spirits roam,
Finding joy far from their home.
Ghosts playing tag with shimmery glee,
Just don't trip over that old tree!

The wind tells stories, soft and light,
Of gnomes and fairies, a wild sight.
They gather to gossip, a nightly spree,
Is that a pumpkin or just me?

With shadows waltzing on the ground,
Laughter and giggles are all around.
A mischievous breeze begins to play,
And steals my hat! No fair, I say!

But here, the mirth is always bright,
In this refuge, we dance with delight.
So raise a glass to the silly things,
And join the fun that this place brings.

Portraits of Light in Evergreen Shadows

In a tree with branches wide,
Squirrels play and often hide.
With acorns tossed from high above,
They giggle and they shove.

A sunbeam dances on the floor,
While rabbits peek out, wanting more.
A grin upon the fox's face,
As everyone joins the silly chase.

The shadows stretch, a stage prepared,
With leafy hats, they are well paired.
Each critter wears a funny tune,
As laughter waltzes 'neath the moon.

The breeze begins to swirl around,
Tickling all who've gathered 'round.
In this realm of light and cheer,
They share the joy, the world is clear.

The Gathering of Stars and Leaves

Beneath the boughs, they spin and twirl,
A band of fun, a raucous whirl.
With leaves like capes, they flutter by,
While crickets chirp a lullaby.

The owls wear glasses, wise and quaint,
Sipping dew like aged saint.
A raccoon juggles shiny stones,
While all the creatures cheer and moan.

Moonlight giggles, tickling toes,
As fireflies join the fun that glows.
Each critter brings their quirkiest task,
In laughter's veil, they all will bask.

In a night so wild, and so absurd,
Not a single truth is heard.
Just joyful pranks and dances free,
An earthbound circus, come and see!

Harmony in the Shade's Lull

In the shade, the wisdom grows,
But chaos reigns where laughter flows.
A hedgehog's hat, a turtle's shoe,
In this strange land, it's all askew.

Bumblebees wear tiny ties,
As they plot schemes in starry skies.
Gossip flies on wings of glee,
While butterflies hold court for free.

The gentle breeze plays pranks galore,
As it opens wide a secret door.
A picnic basket spills its feast,
With stories shared, they laugh, at least.

Harmony sings in shifts of light,
As friends engage in merry fight.
In giggles, the shade feels just right,
A banquet of joy awaits the night.

A Meadow's Dream Beneath the Glade

In a meadow where dreams collide,
A rabbit hops with oodles of pride.
Dancing daisies join the affair,
While a hedgehog spins without a care.

Caterpillars wear party hats,
As butterflies laugh, like silly brats.
The sun beams down with a wink,
While frogs croak tunes, and all can sing.

With every swoosh of gentle wind,
Buttercups glow, their laughter pinned.
Each moment's a jest, a game to cheer,
In this meadow, joy draws near.

Under the glade where dreams unfold,
The laughter of nature is pure and bold.
A whimsical scene, bright and grand,
As the whole world dances hand in hand.

Shelter from the World

In a leafy house where squirrels play,
I dodge the raindrops, hip-hip-hooray!
Bees buzz on jokes, flowers laugh in cheer,
While ants in a line wave, "Have no fear!"

Clouds drip their thoughts like a soggy sponge,
But here I sip tea; I can never grunge.
The world's busy noise is a giggle from afar,
Just me and my snacks under this leafy bar.

A Refuge in Dappled Light

Sunbeams dance like clumsy cats,
I dodge shadow mice, still wearing my hats.
A ladybug serves tea with a tiny grace,
While butterflies tango all over the place.

The sun sneezes bright, oh what a sight,
Leaves shimmy and shake – pure delight!
A picnic of giggles laid out on blades,
With ants as waiters in stylish parades.

Memories Encased in Bark

Bark marks the tales of a hundred years,
Like diaries coated in puddles and tears.
I sketch silly faces on soft, grubby wood,
While the tree whispers tales of misunderstood.

Each knot in the trunk laughs at the past,
Remembering friends from a summer so fast.
A raccoon named Joe dropped his lunch with a thunk,
Now laughter rings out where the shadows have sunk.

How the Wind Whispers Here

The wind flutters by with a mischievous grin,
Tickling my ear while soft tickles begin.
"It's great fun to dance!" it twirls in the air,
Making the leaves snicker without a care.

With every gust, a secret the trees share,
Like whispers of laughter in the warm summer air.
I close my eyes tight, let the chuckles unfold,
In this jovial realm, where wonders are told.

Embraced by Nature's Arms

Beneath the branches, squirrels play,
They dance and prance in a silly way.
While birds recite their morning tunes,
I laugh along with the buzzing loons.

A picnic spread upon the ground,
With ants and bugs that scurry 'round.
They steal my sandwiches, oh what fun,
Nature's creatures, always on the run.

My hat flies off, a gusty trick,
A raccoon steals it—oh, that sly nick!
I chase the critter, my friends in tow,
This tree's a stage, for quite the show!

In nature's arms, where laughter reigns,
Every moment holds sweet refrains.
Life's quirks unfold like the blooming flowers,
Bringing joy and shade in sunny hours.

In the Hollow of Ancient Boughs

In a hollow where shadows softly dwell,
A frog hops in with a splashy yell.
His croak is loud, a joyful cheer,
Bouncing around without any fear.

A picnic basket sits, but oh dear me,
A raccoon sneaks in, as sneaky can be.
He nibbles my cookie, gives me a wink,
It's hard to be mad when he's quicker than a blink.

The boughs above sway, tickling my head,
Sending down twigs like nature's thread.
With giggles that echo and birds in flight,
In moments like these, all feels just right.

Ancient secrets whispered in breeze,
Nature's laughter is sure to please.
With every mishap, joy finds a way,
Under these boughs, let's frolic and play.

Dappled Light and Hidden Dreams

Dappled light dances, playful and bright,
While shadows chase laughter, a curious sight.
The leaves gossip low, as friends gather 'round,
Sharing wild tales in the green playground.

I trip over roots, and the laughter erupts,
As a chipmunk scurries, clearly abrupt.
He stops for a moment, then darts out of sight,
Leaving me chuckling at nature's delight.

A butterfly flutters with elegant flair,
Like it's auditioning for the latest fair.
With each giggle shared, a new tale begins,
In the embrace of nature, everyone wins.

So let's toast to the moments, both silly and sweet,
With flowers for hats and bare dusty feet.
In this patch of joy, with friends oh so dear,
We dance through the light, drinking in cheer.

Beneath the Verdant Veil

Beneath green layers where mischief hides,
A lizard darts out, in colorful strides.
His perch is the twig, his throne quite grand,
As I chuckle, he waves with a cheeky hand.

The breeze carries laughter, swaying the leaves,
While daisies share secrets with playful thieves.
A game of tag with the butterfly troupe,
Around the tree trunk, in giggly loops.

My hat takes flight on the wings of the gale,
The chase that ensues tells quite the tale.
With nature's embrace wrapping us tight,
We dance through the chaos, a pure delight.

So come join the fun where the wild things roam,
With laughter as our sweet, timeless poem.
In this lush canopy, we find our place,
Grinning wide as we bask in grace.

Tales Weaved in Twilit Green

In the shade where squirrels dance,
A rabbit spins a wild romance.
The birds gossip with a twinkling eye,
While shadows peek and whisper, oh my!

A turtle plays the role of a judge,
As crickets argue, there's no grudge.
Leaves shake with laughter, they just can't stop,
In this leafy realm, they pop and bop!

A mushroom wears a hat too tall,
A snail's the star of a comedy ball.
With each tiny step, a giggle erupts,
In twilit green, joy never interrupts.

So gather round, let stories ignite,
In this friendly wood, everything's bright.
The laughter lingers, the fun unfolds,
In tales weaved here, life's never old.

The Embrace of Seasons' Change

Spring arrives with a playful tease,
As flowers grin, swaying in the breeze.
Winter's snowman wears a silly frown,
As he melts gently, falling down town.

Fall gives apples a playful chase,
As pumpkins roll with a jolly face.
The summer sun throws a comical beam,
Making everyone burst at the seam.

With each season's quirky spat,
The critters wiggle, imagine that!
Nature chuckles, a whole troupe of jokes,
As winds carry laughter of all the folks.

So dance in each season, join the play,
In every moment, find joy's display.
For life's a stage with constant range,
In the embrace of seasons' change.

Hushed Voices Among the Foliage

Among the leaves, whispers abound,
Sticks crack jokes without a sound.
A chipmunk says, 'Did you hear that?',
As a loaf of bread rolls past like a cat.

The owls turn with a knowing grin,
As the grasshoppers tap dance, so thin.
A time for laughter, a time for jest,
Nature's stage puts humor to the test.

With every gust, the trees shake with glee,
As laughter dances, wild and free.
A bad pun from the brook makes waves,
While laughter bounces, nature saves.

So hush your heart and lend an ear,
For stories of fun flutter near.
Embrace the joy that nature bequeaths,
In hushed voices, where laughter breathes.

Where Nature's Heart Beats Softly

In the woods where laughter flows,
The critters play, striking silly poses.
Mice wear shoes that are two sizes too big,
And fireflies dance in a boisterous jig.

The sun peeks through, a playful tease,
As rabbits nimbly hop with ease.
Each rustle hints at a brand-new jest,
As the forest throws its merry fest.

The fox sports a hat that's far too wide,
A crow caws out with a comical slide.
Chipmunks chuckle at shadows that prance,
In this whimsical world, all creatures dance.

So lend an ear to nature's soft beat,
Where humor and heart delightfully meet.
In the greenery's quilt of joy and mirth,
Life blooms bright in this chuckling berth.

A Tapestry of Branches and Dreams

In a tree where squirrels plot,
They dance and frolic on their spot.
A whispering breeze gives them a laugh,
As they prepare for nature's craft.

With branches thick and bark so rough,
They gather acorns, yet it's tough.
For every snack that's stashed away,
A hungry bird will steal their play.

The shadows stretch, the sunlight beams,
As daydreams weave through winding schemes.
With laughter shared among the leaves,
They twirl and spin like little thieves.

The Watchful Guardian Above

A wise old tree, with eyes like owls,
Observes the world with chuckling growls.
"What's that, a cat trying to climb?
Here comes a tumble, oh, just in time!"

With branches swaying to and fro,
He chuckles at the antics below.
A dog will dance, then chase its tail,
While the tree shakes leaves and starts to wail.

With every snap of twigs in glee,
The guardian laughs, "Just wait and see!
Life's a jest beneath my crown,
As nature's clowns come tumbling down!"

Comfort Within Nature's Hold

In nature's nook, with roots like hugs,
A seat awaits for weary shrugs.
Come gather round, the shade is grand,
Where laughter blooms across the land.

Beneath the boughs, a picnic spread,
With snacks galore to feast and dread.
"Is that my sandwich?" shouts a bee,
"Or just another ploy to tease me?"

Friends gather close, in games of chase,
With nature's joy, we find our place.
The chuckles rise, where worries fade,
In this embrace, good times invade.

The Echo of Leaves in the Breeze

Leaves rustle loud, like gossiping friends,
They share the tales that never end.
"Did you see that? He missed his perch!
And landed flat with quite a lurch!"

The wind joins in with playful sounds,
As nature laughs and joy abounds.
Each gust a giggle, full of cheer,
Whispers of mischief we all can hear.

In this green hall, the echoes play,
Of silly stunts that made our day.
With each soft brush of air and leaf,
Life's funny moments bring such relief.

The Canopy's Silent Confessions

In a world where squirrels play,
Nutty dreams drift far away.
Whispers linger in the breeze,
As leaves gossip with the bees.

A raccoon dines on fallen snacks,
While owls study their quirks and cracks.
Every rustle tells a tale,
Of mischief caught by daylight's veil.

The branches chuckle, sway, and sway,
A dance of shadows, come what may.
Sunbeams tickle leafy cheeks,
Nature's humor surely speaks.

So gather round, be not so coy,
Join the dance, enjoy the joy.
Nature's laughter fills the glade,
In this wondrous leafy parade.

Serenity Amidst Twisting Branches

Forgotten shoes and lost goldfish,
A tree's complaint, an odd wish.
Twisting limbs and cheeky grins,
Create a stage for light-hearted sins.

A squirrel plots with crafty grace,
Chasing shadows, a wild race.
Falling leaves with gentle plop,
Old branches giggle, 'Don't you stop!'

The sunlight flickers, tempers rise,
A chorus of chirps, no need for lies.
Roots entwine like gossip shy,
While butterflies flutter, oh my oh my!

In this realm of hearty cheer,
Laughter echoes, crystal clear.
For moments stitched in time's embrace,
Are memories that we now chase.

Beneath the Arching Limbs

A grand contest, who can climb high?
A frog croaks softly, "I could fly!"
Twisted roots act as springboards,
While all the critters plot their hoards.

Chirping challenges fill the air,
A worm pokes out without a care.
In this ol' tree, a festive spree,
Where each new branch brings joy, you see.

A toss of nuts from a hidden stash,
Leaves fall, and at times, a crash!
Laughter rings as shadows spill,
And dandelions bend to thrill.

Arched limbs sway in joyful glee,
What a sight, come climb with me!
Nature's court of jesters bright,
Where every day brings pure delight.

Cradled in Nature's Arms

Nestled in this leafy space,
A jolly breeze begins to race.
With every rustle, a playful cheer,
The laughter rings to every ear.

A chipmunk steals a cookie crumb,
While blooms above begin to hum.
They crack jokes, old branches sway,
In this sanctuary, let's all play!

Worms in suits make quite the show,
Wiggle and giggle, fast or slow.
The jester sun peeks through the green,
In this realm, nothing's routine.

So come along, bring your delight,
In nature's arms, all feels right.
With jokes and smiles, our hearts embrace,
In this joyous, warm, green place.

The Quiet Sanctuary Below

A squirrel perched with stylish flair,
Checks its watch and twirls its hair.
Here lies a world of nutty dreams,
Laughter spills like sunlight beams.

The whispers of leaves, the giggles of grass,
Grasshoppers leap in a hasty class.
'Time for lunch!' the bumblebees say,
As they buzz by in a haphazard way.

Crickets chirp with comic intent,
Making sure the laughter's well-spent.
Even the roots seem to dance around,
In this cozy nook where joy can be found.

A funny old dog finds a shady seat,
Watches the antics of all he can greet.
In this silly symphony beneath the green,
Life is a riot, the best yet unseen.

Solace Underneath the Verdant Throne

A parrot squawks jokes, quite a hit,
While a tortoise grins, enjoying the skit.
Rabbits hop in and out of the fun,
Telling tales of races they run.

A snail tells secrets in slow, deep tones,
While a family of mice gathers in groans.
The acorn falls, and a laugh takes flight,
As the frog leaps up with all of its might.

A soft breeze whispers puns to the sky,
As the daisies roll over, giggling, oh my!
Who knew such whimsy could thrive in this place,
With laughter and joy in nature's own space?

Beneath green canopies, the fun never ends,
Where all of the critters are party-time friends.
Each moment here feels like a delightful tease,
As they dance in the sun and wiggle with ease.

Heartbeats in the Shade

Under branches which twist and twine,
A rabbit's joke is the best on the line.
The echoing giggles are hard to suppress,
As they all laugh at the squirrel's nutty dress.

Bumblebees buzz in a harmony sweet,
While the ants march by with their parade of feet.
Every flutter and flurry is laughter in tune,
In the soft, dappled glow of a lazy afternoon.

A woodpecker drums on a tree's rough hide,
Making tunes that build up the fun-filled tide.
A stray cat yawns, rolls over, and grins,
As the antics below spark joy from within.

In this cozy spot where silliness reigns,
The critters unite and forget their mundane pains.
They all share a joy that's simply contagious,
In their secret retreat, hilariously outrageous.

The Longing of Branches Above

Branches sway like they're dancing to tune,
While the raccoons pull pranks beneath the moon.
Laughter peeks out from the nooks and the bends,
As the night unfolds with delightful friends.

The owls hoot jokes in wise, hearty ways,
While the rabbits rejoice in the night's soft haze.
Stars twinkle bright, joining in on their fun,
As the cool night air hints at things still undone.

A wise old tree spins a tall, funny tale,
Of a time when the winds blew hard and pale.
Beneath all the giggles, a mystery sings,
Of the epic shenanigans from all sorts of things.

With every new rustle comes laughter anew,
As night creatures tell tales 'neath the sky's deep blue.
So here is the secret to this gathering's charm,
In this wild space of mirth, there's never a qualm.

A Journey Through Nature's Whispers

Amidst the trees, a squirrel danced,
He wore a hat, and how it pranced.
The branches giggled in delight,
As winds began to blow so tight.

Birds chirped jokes, not very funny,
One said, "I'm no cash cow, honey!"
The flowers laughed, a colorful crew,
While bees debated who was the bee's knees too.

A turtle with a monocle strolled,
Claiming, "I'm the fastest, I'm bold!"
The rabbits snickered, 'That's absurd!'
While him, they dubbed the joking nerd.

The sun peeked down, with a bright grin,
Saying, "I'm just here to let you in!"
So nature chuckled, wild and free,
Creating fun for you and me.

Echoes of Life Among the Greens

In the meadow, a frog did sing,
Claiming himself the next great king.
The grasshoppers laughed, not impressed,
Hopping away, they felt quite blessed.

A tree leaned closer, to hear the chat,
"What's this nonsense? Imagine that!"
The daisies whispered, "What a show!"
As squirrels threw acorns, to and fro.

A bear with spectacles read some gripes,
"Why do humans like to wear stripes?"
The rabbits chuckled, and rolled in glee,
"Pure fashion faux pas, just wait and see!"

Even old rocks had wisecracks to share,
"Life's too short, so don't just stand there!"
In this green haven, laughter runs free,
Echoing joy in nature's decree.

The Peace Found in Nature's Interlace

A lazy dog dreamed under the shade,
Of chasing rabbits, such a grand parade.
Ticks and ants formed a quirky team,
Dancing in rhythm, what a funny dream!

Nearby a snail wore a cape, quite proud,
Claiming, "I'm the fastest in this crowd!"
While fireflies blinked with all their might,
Saying, "We're the stars of the night."

In the bushes, a family of bees,
Held a meeting, buzzing with ease.
"Let's find that nectar, it'll be a feast,"
And one joked, "I hope it's not yeast!"

The trees swayed softly, keeping the beat,
While shadows played hide and seek on the street.
In this garden of whimsy, oh, what a place,
Finding joy in nature's warm embrace.

Stories Nestled in Nature's Arms

A bear told tales of his wild nights,
Of fishing trips and playful fights.
The otters snickered, splashing around,
Saying, "You've never left this ground!"

A fox piped up, with a flick of his tail,
"Life's an adventure, let's set sail!"
While owls perched high, rolled their eyes,
"Where's your ship? Or were those just lies?"

A family of ducks had quite the debate,
"Who's the fastest? Let's set a date!"
While the pond rippled with laughter and sound,
As frogs croaked, "We'll judge from the ground!"

The sun began to set with a grin,
Painting the sky, where stories begin.
In this playful haven, wild and warm,
Nature's tales take shape in every form.

The Heart of the Forest's Embrace

In the shade where squirrels play,
A dog and cat parade each day.
They plot their grand escape from home,
While branches laugh—a leafy dome.

The bird perched high cannot be found,
With funny tales that float around.
The oak is wise, the beech so sleek,
Together, they hold secrets, cheek to cheek.

A rabbit hops, in search of snacks,
While mushrooms giggle at their tracks.
A bear rolls by with slippers on,
He waves to trees—they're never wrong.

The forest whispers quirky jokes,
That tickle roots and jest with folks.
So come and join this jolly prank,
In nature's realm, we all can thank.

Memories Woven in Green Threads

A spider spins a web of dreams,
While breezes tease with gentle beams.
The mice make plans for late-night feasts,
As crickets chirp—those funny beasts.

Leaves dance down in a twirling race,
As a raccoon wears a leaf as lace.
The owl hoots with a quirky cheer,
While hedgehogs giggle, drawing near.

Each plant whispers a tale to share,
Of near-miss dances in the air.
A beetle trips on twigs anew,
They laugh it off, as friends would do.

The woods are rich with jest and play,
Where laughter sparkles every day.
And every creature, big and small,
Weaves memories where fun is all.

Lullabies of the Woodland Flute

A fox plays tunes on a wooden flute,
While rabbits shuffle in a wild pursuit.
The trees sway low, they nod in time,
As fireflies dance in rhythm and rhyme.

The nighttime stars are laughing bright,
As raccoons serenade the night.
The owls hoot a cheerful refrain,
Mixing melodies with the soft rain.

A badger taps his paws with glee,
In joy, the woods become a spree.
Singing along to nature's score,
Each note invites the critters to explore.

So close your eyes and dream away,
For woodland creatures love to play.
With flutes of joy and banter free,
The night unfolds its harmony.

Beneath the Guardian of Time

The grand old tree wears wisdom's crown,
While squirrels chatter, hopping 'round.
Each branch a witness to a jest,
Where laughter's roots are never pressed.

A turtle tries to race a hare,
Both end up lost in laughter's glare.
The leaves applaud, a noisy crush,
As flowers giggle, bask in hush.

With gnarled bark and stories bold,
The tree knows secrets never told.
While shadows play a game of tag,
And sunlight paints its perfect swag.

So gather close, let's share a laugh,
With nature's quirks, we fill our path.
For time with friends beneath the shade,
Turns life into a grand charade.

Sylvan Soliloquies

In a tree so wide and grand,
Where squirrels plot and plan their stand,
The leaves laugh softly, rustle bright,
While birds discuss their fowl delight.

With acorns flying, it's a game,
A nutty jest, who'll take the blame?
A wise old owl hoots in the night,
Calling all critters for a fright.

Beneath the branches, shadows play,
As sunbeam dancers seize the day,
Each critter wears a clever grin,
In nature's sitcom, let's begin!

So gather 'round, oh woodland crew,
It's time to laugh and joke anew,
For life is fleeting, so they say,
In the shade, we frolic, come what may.

Emotions in the Shade's Warmth

Beneath the leaves, where shadows twine,
The breeze brought laughter, oh so fine,
A chipmunk juggles fungi in style,
While a turtle grins, it's been a while.

A bumblebee buzzes with glee,
As butterflies dance—oh, let it be!
No worries here, just fun and cheer,
With Mr. Toad croaking something queer.

The shadows stretch, a playful tease,
As branches wiggle in the breeze,
The world outside may rush and pine,
But here in shade, we sip on wine.

With giggles ringing, hearts shall play,
In this soft haven, come what may,
For all emotions find their flight,
In laughter's glow, by day and night.

Rituals of the Leafy Heart

Each leaf a note in nature's tune,
They wave and sway like a silly cartoon,
A raccoon dons a hat, oh so bright,
As laughter echoes into the night.

Under the boughs, the magic spills,
With antics that cure all the ills,
A waltzing deer with two left feet,
In rhythm, somehow, it's still a treat!

The wind hums softly a wacky song,
As critters join in, where they belong,
They twirl and spin, hoot and chat,
What a grand party! How about that?

With nature clapping, they leap and bound,
In leafy circles, joy is found,
So pause a moment, join the fun,
For in this grove, we're all as one.

Nature's Gentle Guard

In green armor, the tree stands tall,
With branches watching over all,
The laughter of frogs, a nightly show,
As fireflies blink in a soft glow.

A playful breeze brings whispers near,
That tickle the ears and spark good cheer,
A skunk in a top hat makes a fuss,
While raccoons giggle, who'd ride the bus?

In gentle shade, the stories spun,
Of silly things that all were done,
As petals twirl in a light ballet,
Life in the grove dances every day.

So here we gather, come one, come all,
In nature's court, we have a ball,
For joy is found in every part,
Where laughter blooms, with nature's heart.

A Home in the Arms of Nature

In branches high, a squirrel stirs,
Claiming acorns, causing quite a blur.
Nature's laughter fills the air,
While bees dance like they haven't a care.

A picnic chaos, ants on patrol,
Stealing crumbs as they take their toll.
A grumpy toad, he croaks a tune,
While sunbeams wiggle, making us swoon.

Children chase shadows, giggles abound,
Even the grass seems to laugh at the ground.
From buzzing bees to rustling leaves,
Nature's antics are what one believes.

Home is here among the glee,
Where laughter and nature mix joyfully.
In every nook, a story takes flight,
Creating memories, pure delight.

Memories Woven in Green Shadows

In the shade, a cat naps all day,
Dreams of fish that just slip away.
The wind whispers secrets we share,
As petals gossip in midair.

A bug on a leaf strikes a pose,
No one knows where he gets his clothes.
A dance of pollen, a comedy show,
Nature's cast, putting on the grow.

Friends make wishes on dandelion fluff,
But laughter takes over, it's more than enough.
As shadows stretch, we weave our tales,
In this green haven where joy prevails.

Memories lift like a bird in flight,
Every giggle echoing day and night.
In this lively quilt of greens and hues,
Every moment here feels like news.

A Shroud of Environmental Dreaming

A slumbering owl snores in delight,
In mid-snooze, he takes on the night.
While crickets chirp their sleepy songs,
The moon winks at the night's silly wrongs.

Deer prance by, with glittering eyes,
While raccoons plot under starlit skies.
The trees pull their branches in close,
As laughter hangs heavy, more than a boast.

Soft whispers tease the slumbering ground,
With dreams of nuts flipping round and round.
Fireflies flash in a bright ballet,
In this nighttime frolic, we laugh and play.

Here dreams wrap like a leafy shield,
Every giggle, a joyous yield.
In the stillness, we find our schemes,
Casting silly, nocturnal dreams.

Secrets Spun in Leaf Shadows

Beneath the foliage, secrets creep,
Where chatter bugs buzz, and time takes a leap.
Frogs quack jokes; the sunlight agrees,
Leaving us chuckling on our knees.

A feathered friend shakes a tailfeather,
As if making fun of rain or good weather.
Bees debating which flower to pick,
Arguing quite loudly, Nature's own shtick.

The sun pops out to steal a glance,
Watching limbs jiggle in a leafy dance.
While shadows weave, the stories unfold,
In this haven of laughter, sweet and bold.

Every rustle tells tales of the day,
In the green embrace, whimsy holds sway.
Secrets are spun, crafted with glee,
In this tapestry of joyous decree.

The Elder's Gentle Embrace

In the shade of a tree, soft and wide,
A squirrel sneezes, and what a pride!
The leaves all chuckle, a rustling song,
While bees do the cha-cha, all day long.

Old Oak grumbles, 'These folks are quite mad!'
His branches wobble, they surely look bad.
Yet all the critters, in laughter, unite,
In nature's circus, every day's bright.

Treetop Murmurs in the Stillness

The birds gossip wildly, oh what a chat,
'Did you see Bunny? He's wearing a hat!'
A worm adds, 'Did he pay for that style?'
While ants march in line, with a dubious smile.

The wind whispers secrets, all light and quick,
The old trunk chuckles, with a gentle flick.
All critters listen, in utter delight,
As shadows dance boldly, from morning till night.

Cradle of Sunlight and Shade

A cozy nook where the sunlight peeks,
A lazy lizard dreams, or so it seems.
Grasshoppers giggle, their legs all a-bop,
While daisies join in, and never do stop.

The shadows play tag, oh what a silly game,
Yet the ants march on, focused, no shame.
The laughter of nature echoes around,
In this joyful haven, where fun knows no bound.

Reverie in the Shade of Giants

Beneath massive trunks, the critters convene,
Debating the best way to pick a green bean.
A squirrel shouts, 'I'll make my own stew!'
But ends up with acorns, and some mountain dew.

The sunbeams giggle, as they filter down,
Tickling the toad who's lost in his frown.
In this peaceful circus, up high and low,
Every leaf has a story, every shadow a show.

Secrets of the Leafy Watcher

A squirrel steals snacks from a picnic plate,
Guarded by branches, he thinks he's quite great.
Caught in the act, he freezes so still,
Eyes wide as saucers, a true comedy thrill.

Birds gossip above about his bold thievery,
Chirping in chorus, they share the big mystery.
"Did you see him dash? Oh, what a sight!"
A nut in his paw, he'd fled in delight.

Rabbits on the ground chuckle at the scene,
"He thinks he's a thief, but he's just a functioning machine!"
Whispers of the boughs join in on the jest,
Nature's laughter echoes, a comedic fest.

Even the leaves shimmy in playful cheer,
While shadows dance, drawing close the near.
A spectacle unfolds in the dappled light,
Where nature brings drama, oh what a night!

Dance of the Swaying Boughs

Branches bend low for a whimsical sway,
Where the breeze teases and children will play.
A crow gets dizzy, spinning round and round,
This feathered ballet is the talk of the town.

Acorns drop like rain as the tree laughs loud,
Creating a ruckus, it's gathering a crowd.
"Look out below!" cries a nutty aide,
But they all take cover; no one's afraid.

A ladybug jives with a snail on the side,
Underneath this greenery, they let laughter collide.
With every wiggle, the world seems bright,
As nature hums tunes, a sheer delight.

Even the shadows sway to the beat,
While the sun winks down at this lively treat.
In this leafy dance, who could feel glum?
Together they frolic, inviting us to come!

Beneath the Expansive Green Mantle

Frogs in tuxedos leap with flair,
Ribbiting jokes like they've no care.
The grass tickles toes as they make their rounds,
Under this green cloak, all joy abounds.

Bumbling bees swagger with style so bold,
Buzzing sweet verses, their stories unfold.
Mocking the flowers that bloom at their feet,
Nature's comedy is truly a treat.

A hedgehog rolls in a quirky parade,
As critters assemble, none are afraid.
With twigs for trombones and nuts as their drums,
Every moment here brings forth giggles and hums.

Caterpillars wiggle, trying to dance,
While butterflies chuckle at their clumsy chance.
In this wild realm, where laughter flows free,
The charm of the green makes it all seem like glee!

Embraced by Nature's Veil

Dandelions bloom in a cheeky display,
Winking at passersby, brightening their day.
With every soft breeze, they giggle and twirl,
These wild little jesters, give life a whirl.

A mischievous rabbit hops in delight,
With floppy ears bouncing, oh what a sight!
He tripped on a root, and what a grand fall,
The shrubbery chuckles, in its leafy hall.

Bees throw a party, pollens galore,
While crickets provide beats, oh, what a score!
Every critter in tow, singing tunes of fun,
Nature's wide stage, where all are welcome to run.

As shadows stretch long and the sun starts to fade,
The laughter continues, a grand masquerade.
In this charming embrace, where jokes take flight,
Every moment is magic, filled with sheer delight!

Tales of Timeless Trunks

In a grove where laughter flows,
Squirrels in tuxedos strike a pose.
They dance around the roots so wide,
Throwing acorns like confetti, with pride.

A rabbit with a monocle, so spry,
Tells tales of how he learned to fly.
While birds in bow ties sing so sweet,
As they tap their tiny dancing feet.

The wise old owl gives a knowing nod,
As squirrels debate if nuts are flawed.
With each silly thought, the trees do sway,
In this lively theater of woodland play.

At dusk, the party winds down slow,
With moonlight shining on the show.
A final dance, a last hooray,
Then all curl up 'til the break of day.

A Haven in Canopied Dreams

Beneath the leaves, a cozy nest,
A squirrel thinks he's quite the best.
With dreams of cheese and nuts galore,
His friends just laugh, "You want more?"

A hedgehog juggles acorns round,
While birds debate who makes the sound.
Chirps and chuckles fill the air,
As laughter dances everywhere.

A wise old tortoise takes his time,
To share a joke, it's all in rhyme.
His friends just roll and laugh so hard,
For punchlines come from his backyard.

As stars peek through the leafy space,
They settle down, each in their place.
With giggles low and dreams so bright,
They drift away into the night.

Whispers Beneath the Ancient Canopy

In the shade, secrets do reside,
Where all the critters love to bide.
A gopher tells the funniest tale,
Of how he tried to ride a snail.

The raccoons sneak in, all in a row,
To join in the fun, just to steal the show.
With masks and capes, they prance about,
With plans so silly, they roam about.

A frog on a lily pad does leaps,
While chattering owls swap funny peeps.
In this enchanted world, laughter blends,
With stories shared among the friends.

As shadows stretch and stars ignite,
They giggle softly, what a night!
With dreams of mischief, they all agree,
Tomorrow brings more fun, oh me!

Shadows of Tender Serenity

In the hush, a shadow winks,
While squirrels plot and share their kinks.
A chipmunk wearing tiny shoes,
Plans a race but starts to snooze.

A playful breeze joins in the fun,
As whispers swirl 'round everyone.
The turtles laugh, they're moving slow,
"Who knew our shadows could steal the show?"

With raindrops falling, they scat and slip,
Chasing shadows as they flip.
A game of tag that no one wins,
Just laughter, giggles, hugs, and grins.

As twilight settles, light begins to fade,
Their playful hearts happily invade.
Together they bask in the soft moonlight,
Dreams of laughter in a world so bright.

Whispers Beneath the Canopy

In the shade where squirrels chat,
A raccoon wears a sunhat.
The birds gossip and sing with glee,
While ants march forth, as busy as can be.

A breeze tickles leaves overhead,
While chipmunks dance, no fear or dread.
The shadows play like silly clowns,
In this leafy stage where laughter abounds.

A picnic's set, but oh dear me!
A sandwich flew, oh what a spree!
The laughter travels far and wide,
As sticky fingers slip and slide.

So here we sit, in giggles lost,
With nature's fun, we pay no cost.
In this green world where joy ignites,
Life's a laugh, with endless delights.

Secrets of the Shaded Grove

In shadows deep where mischief reigns,
A frog leaps in and squeaks his gains.
The turtles wear their glasses tight,
Debating whose shell is more bright.

The rabbits throw a silent rave,
While hedgehogs dance, so fresh and brave.
A whispered joke from tree to tree,
As every critter giggles free.

The wise old owl rolls his big eyes,
As sneaky squirrels spin their lies.
A watermelon spills, what a sight!
Fun on the grass, till the stars ignite.

In this grove where secrets fly,
The tales grow wings and soar up high.
We trade our cares for a silly song,
In this embrace where we belong.

Cradle of Leaves and Memories

In the cradle where memories dwell,
A snail leaves trails like stories to tell.
The fireflies wink, all blinking bright,
While mice play cards in the warm moonlight.

A rustling leaf talks back with sass,
As mushrooms giggle, a fun little class.
The grass tickles toes, a playful fuss,
While playful jesters make a big fuss.

Laughter bubbles in the air so sweet,
As squirrels chase round their little beat.
A secret stash of acorns galore,
In this leafy playground, who could ask for more?

As night draws near, we share a grin,
In cases of laughter, we hold our kin.
This cradle of joy, wild and free,
Where every moment's a jubilee.

The Shade's Soft Serenade

In soft shade where shadows prance,
A worm plays tunes that make you dance.
The wind hums low, a playful tease,
While bees buzz round, with sticky knees.

A lizard croons, his voice so smooth,
As butterflies join, in elegant groove.
The petals sway with colors bright,
In this serenade of pure delight.

A tumbleweed rolls, with laughter so bold,
While crickets narrate tales of old.
The sun dips low, a funny sight,
In this gathering of giggles, into the night.

With each soft note, our cares take flight,
In the magic of shade, so warm and bright.
We'll cherish the fun, the joy we made,
In this charming woods, where worries fade.

Tranquility Beneath Twisted Limbs

A squirrel stole my sandwich, oh what a sight,
I waved goodbye as he took flight.

The wind played games, tickled my nose,
While bees in suits prepared for shows.

Laughter echoed as branches swayed,
Nature's stand-up, and I was amazed.

With every rustle, secrets were shared,
In this goofy haven, I was quite scared.

Where Roots Cradle Time

Roots like arms they hug the ground,
In their embrace, lost treasures are found.

Time ticked slow, like molasses in sun,
With friendly shadows, we had our fun.

A snail declared he'd win the race,
But I left him laughing at his slow pace.

As laughter rang through each twisting vine,
I'd bet my shoes he'd never cross the line!

The Embrace of Wonder Above

Oh look! A bird with a silly hat,
Sang a tune that made me laugh and clap.

Leaves giggled softly, a rustling cheer,
As I danced round, my worries disappeared.

Clouds peeked in, whispering what's next,
Their fluffy jokes left me feeling perplexed.

In this crazy, leafy hall of fame,
I found pure joy in nature's game.

Leafy Lullabies at Dusk

As dusk fell down, the leaves sang low,
   Telling tales of their friends in tow.

A mischievous breeze tossed them about,
An acorn chuckled, "What's that about?"

Night creatures joined in with tunes so bright,
   Singing softly, bringing the moonlight.

With every chorus, a giggle flowed,
In the twilight glow, joy overflowed.

www.ingramcontent.com/pod-product-compliance
Lightning Source LLC
Chambersburg PA
CBHW071651220426
43209CB00100BB/111